DEMON WORSHIP
AND
OTHER SUPERSTITIONS
IN
CEYLON

A *Billa* used by Kattadiyas to frighten ignorant Sinhalese into the performance of ceremonies.

DEMON WORSHIP
AND
OTHER SUPERSTITIONS
IN
CEYLON

GYAN

Published by

Gyan Publishing House
5, Ansari Road
Daryaganj, New Delhi-110002
Phone: 011-47034999, 9811692060
E-mail: books@gyanbooks.com

Distribution Network
gyanbooks.com
India, USA, Canada, UK, Australia, France

ISBN : 978-81-212-3301-9 (PB)
First Published, Madras, 1891

2nd Impression 2020

Printed at: Gyan Press, Delhi.

**Demon Worship and other Superstitions
in
Ceylon**

DEMON WORSHIP

AND

OTHER SUPERSTITIONS

IN

CEYLON.

DEVIL DANCER'S MASK.

MADRAS:

THE CHRISTIAN VERNACULAR EDUCATION SOCIETY.

M. E. PUBLISHING HOUSE, VEPERY.

1891.

CONTENTS.

	Page
Beauty and Fertility of Ceylon	1
Cause of Unhappiness to the Sinhalese	1
Evils of Demon Worship, etc.	3
Origin of Demon Worship	6
Supposed Effects of Demons and Charms. ...	7
Uselessness of Charms and Demon Ceremonies ...	9
Horn-pulling...	13
Possession	14
Kapuism	15
Astrology	16
Omens...	20
The Evil Eye	22
Causes of Sickness	23
Conduct in Time of Sickness	24
How to prevent Fear of Demons	25
Duty of Educated Sinhalese	26
List of Publications	28

CONTENTS

DEMON WORSHIP

AND

OTHER SUPERSTITIONS

IN

CEYLON.

BEAUTY AND FERTILITY OF CEYLON.

CEYLON is one of the most beautiful islands in the world. From early times it has been celebrated as LANKA, "The Resplendent." It is famous for its rubies, sapphires, and pearls. The whole Island is covered with rich vegetation. The forests yield teak, satin wood, calamander and other trees useful for their timber; there are millions of cocoa-nut trees, valuable for many purposes. The fields produce rice and other grains; pepper, cinnamon and cardamoms, give flavour to food; coffee and tea are produced in large quantities; plantains, oranges, mangoes, &c., are plentiful. Cattle, buffaloes, sheep, and goats are numerous, and Ceylon is noted for its elephants.

The heat is not so great as on the neighbouring coast of India, and the rainfall, usually abundant, makes the Island beautifully green all the year round.

CAUSE OF UNHAPPINESS TO THE SINHALESE.

The Sinhalese, living in such a beautiful country, supplied with every thing needful for human wants, should enjoy great happiness. There is, however, one great hindrance to this, which tends to embitter their life, and keeps them in constant terror.

The Emperor of Russia is one of the most powerful and richest monarchs in the world. He has magnificent palaces filled with the most costly furniture; all the luxuries in the world are at his command. His position, however, is not to be envied. He is in constant fear of his life. Armed soldiers have to watch him day and night; even when he travels by rail, sentries have to be stationed at short distances all along the line. His father was murdered when driving through the streets of his capital, and lately a similar attempt was made upon himself.

The Sinhalese, from childhood to their dying day, are kept in somewhat similar dread. There are no persons seeking to shoot them or blow up their houses with gunpowder; but they suppose that there are numbers of evil spirits constantly surrounding them, lurking in the rocks, trees, and jungles, seeking to do them harm. They think that there are gods and goddesses, like Katragam and Pattini, who require to be propitiated: They dare not do certain things because the planets are supposed to be unfavourable; their fields and fruit trees may be blasted by the evil eye; the howling of a dog or the sight of an empty pot may make them miserable for a whole day. No man is without enemies, whom he suspects to be seeking to injure him or even cause his death by *huniyan, angam* or *pilli* charms.

The Sinhalese foolishly believe that by flattery or force they can compel powerful demons to obey them. They offer to them little bits of flesh and other articles which even a beggar would despise. They think them so stupid as to be deceived by the silliest tricks.

The following are some of the ceremonies performed: Throwing cocoa-nuts, horn-pulling, village dancing, offerings to devalas, huniyan kæpeema, dewol samayama, rata yakun-samayama, sanni-samayama, gará yakuna, Kumára-pidenna, metiata-pæraweema, nul-bendeema, yantra-bendeema, tel-metireema, kappitawa-dánedeema, attagaha metireema, bali-ereema, pirit keema, &c., &c.

There is this great difference between the Emperor of Russia and the Sinhalese,—that the dangers from which the former has to guard against are real, while the latter are terrified by beings which have no existence. Sinhalese frighten their children by saying that *billas* will take them. The parents do not believe that there are *billas*, but the children do. Just as the children are deceived, so the parents, in turn, are deceived by kattadiyas, who tell them that there are demons who must be propitiated by ceremonies. These demons, like the *billas*, have no existence, but they serve to frighten ignorant grown-up Sinhalese.

Evils of Demon Worship, etc.

Besides the constant fear already mentioned, belief in demons leads to other great evils, some of which will be mentioned :

1. **Useless Expense.**—Nearly every ceremony requires to be paid for, some of them at a high rate. When there is sickness in a house, the income may be less, from the men being unable to work, while the expenses are increased. Money, especially in such cases, should not be spent needlessly. Just as pigs, hares, birds, &c., seek to prey upon fields and gardens, so do thousands of kattadiyas, yakaduras, kapuas, astrologers, &c., try to take the money of ignorant people without doing them any good in return.

2. **Increase of Sickness.**—There is now much less sickness in England than there was formerly, and people live several years longer. Ague fever is unknown in districts where it was once very common ; very few die of small-pox ; formerly there were houses for lepers in the principal cities ; now there is not one. How was all this brought about ?

Marshes and bad water are the chief causes of fever ; by draining the marshes and providing good water, fever has been removed ; vaccination is a safeguard against small-pox ; better food and greater cleanliness have put an end to leprosy.

In Ceylon, ignorant people, instead of seeking to prevent sickness by such means, resort to useless ceremonies, so that disease goes on spreading.

Devil ceremonies tend to increase sickness by the encouragement they give to ignorant doctors. In England no man is allowed to practise as a physician till he has passed an examination and got a certificate. In Ceylon a man may set up as a doctor as easily as he can open a shop. When ignorant doctors, from their want of skill, cannot cure a patient, they lay the blame on demons or on some enemy, and this excuse is accepted. With good doctors, many would be cured who now die.

The body is weakest and the causes of disease strongest at night. Exposure to the night air and fatigue sometimes make the sick person worse, or even cause his death. Ceremonies at night tend to spread sickness among all who take part in them.

3. **Quarrels.**—These are often a consequence of the belief in charms. One family lives in bitter enmity with another, all their respective relations and friends ranged on one side, and each trying to injure the other in every possible way by litigation, perjury, theft, and assault sometimes even ending in murder, and such feuds may reach from one generation to another.

The following are examples :

The bridegroom in a marriage procession was dressed like a modliar. The thick clothing, to which he was unaccustomed, the heat and the excitement, made him faint by the way. It was supposed to be caused by some *angam.* The thick velvet coat was taken off and the shirt collar opened. A kattadiya then muttered his charms over a cup of water, part of which was afterwards sprinkled on the bridegroom's face and part poured down his throat. The man soon revived, the kattadiya claiming that it was through his charming. Meanwhile the relations of the bridegroom vowed vengeance against the supposed enemy who had brought this *angam* upon him.

Some time ago there was a lawsuit between two men. Before the case was decided, one of them happened to fall from a cocoa-nut tree, and died instantly. It was imputed to a *huniyan* charm, and deadly hatred arose between the two families.

A young man who promised to become a popular astrologer fell sick and died. His father suspected that another astrologer, who lived in the same village, had practised *huniyan* charms against his son. He borrowed a gun from a neighbour, pretending that it was to drive away some monkeys from a mango tree in his garden. One evening, as the young astrologer was going home along a footpath with thick jungle on each side, he was shot by somebody hidden among the bushes, and died in a few hours. The evidence was not sufficient to convict the old man, but all the villagers knew that he was the murderer.

4. **Moral Degradation.**—There is a Sanskrit proverb, "As is the god, so is the worshipper." We tend to become like those whom we worship. Demons are supposed to be malicious beings, hating what is good, and delighting to injure others. The Sinhalese are naturally gentle, but demon worship fosters evil passions. In one of the *huniyan* charms, the following prayer is made to a she-demon with regard to a supposed enemy: "Eat his flesh and drink his blood. Eat his bones, and muscles and nerves. Drink his heart's blood and suck his marrow. Eat his liver and lungs and entrails." Whether a man is a Buddhist or a Christian, to offer such a prayer is a great sin. There is no she-demon to fulfil such a horrible request: the mischief falls upon the head of the man who utters it. It makes him like a demon. He who paid him to repeat it is equally guilty. People who try to injure others do most harm to themselves.

5. **The Punishment due to Rebellion.**—A wise, good and rightful king demands the obedience of his subjects. Suppose some of his people should set up a low, vile man as their king, they would justly be punished for rebellion. God is the Creator and

rightful Lord of this world. He first gave us life; He keeps us in life; we live on His earth; everything we have belongs to Him. He justly claims our obedience. But demon-worshippers disregard His commands, and honour evil spirits instead of Himself. They deserve the severest punishment.

English people sometimes put brass collars round the necks of their dogs, with their names on them, showing that the dogs are their property. Persons who wear charms show that they have forsaken God, and given themselves up to cruel demons.

Origin of Demon Worship.

Demon worship is the religion of savages. There are islands to the present day inhabited by people like the early Sinhalese. Many uncivilised nations do not believe in natural death. If a man, however old, dies, without being wounded, they conclude that he must have been the victim of charms. In some islands in the Pacific Ocean, pain, through sickness, is supposed to be caused by a demon gnawing the inside of the body. Among the Kafirs of South Africa, if a person gets sick, it is believed that some enemy has bewitched him, and a witch-doctor is employed to "smell out" the man who has done the injury. Until this is done, no one expects him to get better. No medicine is given; they have only charms. Once a chief got a bad cold. A witch-doctor said it was caused by a poor old man, who was at once killed.

It is believed that persons who have met with a violent death and men notorious for crime, become demons, delighting to harm the living. A wicked British officer, killed in Travancore, was supposed to become a demon, and offerings were made at his grave of brandy and cheroots which he loved in life. They were, however, afterwards drunk and smoked by those who presented them.

In a country in Northern Asia, devil priests pretend that demons cause harm by entering the body as stones or thorns. They hide them in their dress beforehand, and after certain ceremonies pretend to suck them out, showing them as proofs of what they say. As they are paid so much for each, they sometimes claim to have brought half a dozen out of a man's stomach.

The first inhabitants of Ceylon were very rude, little better than savages. They were called *yakkhos,* not because they were demons, but because they were demon-worshippers. That they were only ordinary men and women, is shown by Wijeyo and his companions intermarrying with them and having children, just as is the case with foreigners at present.

There is a saying that a wooden vessel long retains the flavour of the liquid with which it was first filled. Most Sinhalese still cling to demon worship, the original superstition of the Island. From the Tamils they learned the worship of the Hindu gods; astrology and Buddhism were also introduced. Buddha, in the *Tun Pitaka,* calls divination, omens, charms, &c., "low arts and lying practices." According to Buddhism, things happen according to *karma,* not on account of the planets or charms. But the Sinhalese mix up demon worship, kapuism, astrology and Buddhism, although contradictory. Buddha, Brahma, Vishnu, and demons are sometimes invoked in the same charm.

Sir Emerson Tennant says in his book on Ceylon, that "their demon ceremonies are performed with observances so barbarous as to be the most revolting evidence still extant of the uncivilised habits of the Sinhalese." (Vol. 1. p. 541). Only a few are yet sufficiently enlightened to see the folly and evil of such customs. This little book is intended to show that they are useless, and ought at once to be given up.

Supposed Effects of Demons and Charms.

If a man gets sick and feels thirst accompanied by great heat in the blood; if he is troubled with frightful dreams; if he raves and talks senselessly; if the disease does not yield to medicine; if while climbing a tree he falls: in many cases all these are supposed to be caused by demons or *huniyan*. This is especially the case if the person has an enemy among his neighbours.

It will first be shown that all these may arise from natural causes.

Let a man take plenty of indigestible food at night, and he will see horrible things in his dreams, if he has not even an attack of cholera.

It is supposed that we think by means of the brain. When it is in good order, a person talks rationally; if a man gets a severe blow on the head, he becomes insensible.

When the brain gets much inflamed, a person loses his senses. If arrack is thrown into the eyes, they become red. The same effect is produced upon the brain when arrack is drunk. The drunken man talks nonsense, and does not know what he is doing. Sometimes great drunkards become like madmen. They cry out with fear, supposing that snakes are crawling over them, or that dreadful faces are grinning at them.

The eyes may get inflamed by disease as well as by having arrack thrown on them, and so may the brain. In strong fever, the brain, as well as the rest of the body, has a burning heat. If very severe, the person becomes delirious.

Just as there may be a boil on the arm or leg while the rest of the body is well, so the brain alone may be affected, and a person may become mad.

If you suddenly twist your foot, you sprain it; if you carry too heavy a load, you may injure your back; if you look at the sun shining in its strength, you will hurt your eyes. In like manner, any sudden strong feeling may harm the brain. People have become insane through the loss at once of all their property. An ayah held a child over deep water, threatening to throw it in. When it came home, it would start up and cry out; it had lost its senses. Thoughtless boys have been known to make a figure of sticks, cover it with white cloth, expose it in a dark night, and so frighten children that they have become insane for a time.

The Sinhalese, from childhood, are in dread of demons. When walking alone in the twilight, they are very apt to fancy that some object they do not see distinctly is an evil spirit. They may become so terrified as to lose their senses. This is especially the case if the place is supposed to be haunted.

Pregnant women are thought to be peculiarly liable to suffer from demons. It is considered necessary to have charms to ensure safe delivery.

If the womb has not sufficient strength to bring forth, it is supposed that some ceremony is needed. In such cases, English doctors, instead of charms, give a medicine which has the property of making the womb draw together, and the child is born.

Women are most afraid of the *Reeri Yakka*, the blood demon, that causes the flow of blood after childbirth. Sometimes the blood fills the womb, and the woman dies. The true *Reeri Yakka* is the ignorant midwife. The very bad custom prevails with them of tearing away the after-birth as soon as the child is born. This causes a flow of blood from the blood vessels. With a good midwife, no *Reeri Yakka* gives any trouble.

People in England get ill, have frightful dreams, and are sometimes killed by accident, just like the Sinhalese. No person in England, however, attributes these things to charms. They are believed to arise from natural causes. The same explanation is given in the best medical books among the Sinhalese, and by intelligent men among them.

Uselessness of Charms and Demon Ceremonies.

It should be clearly understood that God has given certain properties to bodies which act without charms, and cannot be altered by charms. Fire burns, pepper is hot, vinegar is sour, arrack intoxicates, arsenic kills. Suppose a man charmed some water before taking a drink to quench his thirst or a woman charmed some salt before putting it into the pot, even a Sinhalese would laugh at them as fools. They know that they would act without charms. But it is just as absurd to think that charms are necessary in the case of medicines. Castor oil, mercury, and other drugs act from their own nature, just like water or salt. When any one says that charms are also needed, he only shows his ignorance. Any doctor recommending them should be dismissed, and a skilful one employed who does not believe in such nonsense.

Suppose a Sinhalese mother cries out, "Come, *billa*, and take away this child," she knows very well that no one will come. Why? Because there is no such being. Suppose a *billa* charm should be carefully prepared, with suitable offerings, and a man should say, "O great *billa*, kill my enemy, drink his blood, suck his marrow," would this have any effect? None whatever. There is no *billa* to do these things. In like manner *huniyan*, *angam* and *pilli* charms have no effect, because there are no such beings as *Reeri Yakka, Moha Sona Yakka,** *Maha Cola Sanni Yakka,*† &c. They are the inventions of kattadiyas, yakaduras, and others to frighten Sinhalese into performing ceremonies by which they make their living. To invoke them is just as vain as to call upon *billas*.

Folly and Trickery connected with Demon Worship.—Some of the ceremonies are very absurd. They are performed to drive away a devil, but the kattadiya invites all the devils to come from the eight quarters. If a pariah dog got into my house and I wished to put it out, I should not call all the pariah dogs in the village to come.

Attempts are made to cheat the demon. The yakadura sometimes personates the sick man and pretends to die. He is then carried with lamentation, and supposed to be buried. At other times a rude

*Great Graveyard Demon. †Great Demon of Fatal Diseases.

image is made and treated similarly. These people must suppose the demon to be more stupid than a crow, for it knows the difference between a living and dead man, between a corpse and a bundle of sticks.

When thieves wish to steal fruit, they sometimes at night make a wailing cry. The owner, supposing it to be *Bodirimaw*, locks himself up in his house, and the thieves take away loads of plantains at their leisure.

When a person gets sick, a kattadiya often says that some one has practised *huniyan* against him, made an image, pierced it with nails of five metals, and buried it. The kattadiya promises, for a good present, through his ceremonies, to discover the image, and cause the death of the enemy who made it. Pretending to be inspired by the demon, he says, "Go and dig at such a place and you will find the image." The people do so eagerly, find the image, and praise the skill of the kattadiya. The explanation is simple. The kattadiya himself buried the image before the commencement of the ceremony.

At another time the kattadiya pretends to expel the demon by his charms. He orders him away, speaking very boldly. The demon is frightened, and promises to leave. The kattadiya asks for a sign that the promise will be kept. The demon says that he will break the branch of such and such a tree. The people run to the tree and find the branch broken. This is looked upon as a proof that the demon has left the sick person, and the kattadiya receives a handsome present. The truth is that the kattadiya himself broke the branch before the ceremony.

Alleged Power of Charms.—People tell wonderful tales about the cures and injuries supposed to have been wrought by demon ceremonies. As a rule, those who relate them only report what they heard from others. Often they are said to have taken place years ago.

It is, however, quite possible that some persons should recover after the performance of ceremonies,

A woman gets a headache. A charm is muttered, a thread knotted seven times, dyed with saffron, tied on the woman, and she recovers. But so she would if no thread had been tied. After a little rest, most headaches pass away.

The case has been mentioned of the bridegroom who fainted during the marriage procession. When a person faints, the best course is to loose his clothes, especially about the neck, and to sprinkle cold water on his face. In this way he recovers without any charm.

If a fish bone sticks in a person's throat, he may make a ball of rice, repeat a charm over it, and then swallow the rice. Another, if he sprains his foot, charms some oil, rubs it on the part affected, and, by and by, it gets better. Ignorant people suppose the charms are also needed, but the rice ball and the oil would be equally effectual without them.

People get better from most diseases. A person may have ten or even twenty illnesses during his life-time before his death. Some diseases require a certain time to run their course. A boil takes some days to burst, but when it does so, the person gets relief. If ceremony after ceremony is performed, the sick man generally recovers in the end, and the kattadiya takes the credit. If he dies, the kattadiya says that his time had come, when nothing could save him.

Challenge to Kattadiyas.—*Angam* and *pilli* charms are supposed to be very powerful. *Huniyans* may not cause death for months; *angams* are said to be fatal within 7 hours, the person throwing up blood through the nose and mouth.

Again and again kattadiyas have been challenged to do any harm to a person by *angams* or any other charms. Those of the Southern Province are considered the most skilful. A notice was widely circulated, offering a reward of about 200 rupees on the 17th September, 1880, to any kattadiya at Matara who would injure a person by his charms. One or two kattadiyas, who had made great preparations, came forward. A Sinhalese stood before them, while they muttered their charms and burnt resin. At last they blew at him. The man who stood should have fallen down insensible, the blood gushing from his nose and mouth. Instead of that, he burst out laughing. He told the kattadiyas that perhaps they had made some mistake in repeating their charms; so they should try again. They did so, but with the like result, and they were glad to slink away amid the jeers of the people.

Afterwards the same offer was made at Colombo, Kandy, Galle, and Matara; but not one kattadiya came forward. The same sum will be given at the present time to any kattadiya who succeeds.

Some Sinhalese say that kattadiyas now are not skilful, but in former times they could do wonders. It may be asked why, then, did the Sinhalese kings not destroy by charms the Tamils when, more than a thousand years ago, they ravaged parts of Ceylon, burning down the villages and killing the people? Nearly 400 years ago the Portuguese took some of the coast districts of Ceylon: why were they not destroyed by charms? Two hundred years later, why were the same means not employed against the Dutch? In 1848 a pretender tried to raise a rebellion at Matalé. He said that he would charm the guns of the English, so that the bullets would not do any harm; but at the first fire several of his men were shot dead.

The most powerful charms cannot hurt even a fly; they have no power whatever. Only simpletons are deceived by the wonderful stories which kattadiyas tell to get a living.

HORN-PULLING.

This superstitious ceremony is performed when pestilential diseases prevail in the country.

Two parties, upper and lower, go with horns to a certain place, where a kind of altar is erected and other preparations made. The kapua and pattinihamy attend, one joining the upper side, the other the lower. Food is prepared in abundance. After the kapua and pattinihamy have eaten as much as they can, the rest of the provisions is consumed by the people.

First young lads pull with crooked sticks. Next they take small deer-horns, then strong and large ones, some of which are valued at 20 Rupees. Every time a horn is broken, tom-toms are beaten, boys cry out *hiyo, hiyo!* and the conquerors, with obscene language and gestures, insult and ridicule the opposite party.

Gammadu, or Village Dance, often follows Horn-pulling or Breaking of Cocoa-nuts.

It is strange how any person in his senses can believe that horn-pulling, with filthy language, can stop pestilence. It shows what fools there are among the Sinhalese. Even for no other reason than the good name of the nation, such silly practices should be stopped.

Possession.

Pessession means the supposed entrance of a demon into a person. This generally happens in the case of women, most of them are even more ignorant and superstitious than the men. They are weaker, and their bodies are more liable to disease. When not in good health, they sometimes laugh or cry without any apparent reason, and do other strange things. This happens occasionally in England. It is called *hysteria*, and is described in medical books, with the proper treatment.

When women in Ceylon are thought to be possessed, the great recourse is to the temple of Alutnuwara, 11 miles from Kandy: The journey and change of air are often beneficial. If the woman says that the demon will not go away from her, the kapua beats her mercilessly with a stout cane, till he promises to leave.

She and her friends then return home, pleased with the success of the journey.

A man in the Western Province, seeing his wife beginning to show signs of demon possession, immediately seized the house broom, and with it gave her 20 or 30 smart blows, crying out aloud, "Is there a greater demon here than myself? I will teach thee, demon, who I am." This treatment effected a cure.

Madness takes different forms Sometimes a person who has lost his senses supposes himself to be a king. Possession is one variety, especially among superstitious women. If not cured at home, they should be sent to a lunatic asylum.

KAPUISM.

As already mentioned, demon worship first prevailed among the Sinhalese. Some of the kings came from India, and many of them got their wives from that country. Hence the worship of the Hindu gods was mixed up with demon worship and Buddhism.

The gods of which the kapuas are the priests are not thought to possess such evil dispositions as the demons, but they are worshipped for protection against and for the cure of certain diseases.

Small-pox was so fatal in Ceylon that it is called *maha leda,* the great sickness. In India it is thought to be caused by goddess *Mariamman,* the Mother of Death. She is supposed, for her pleasure, to scatter the seeds of the disease. In Ceylon it is attributed to the goddess Pattini.

In Europe small-pox was formerly very deadly. It sometimes swept away the entire inhabitants of a city, and blinded or disfigured one-fourth of the whole population.

Nearly a hundred years ago, an English physician discovered that vaccination prevents small-pox. If properly done, only a very few persons take the disease, and that in a mild form. There are now very few deaths from it in England.

There is no such being as Pattini. Small-pox is neither caused nor cured by her. Offerings to her are perfectly useless. The great safeguard against small-pox is to get children vaccinated. Care should be taken that the little boils which form on the arm are not broken or the effect will be lost. Some people do not believe in vaccination, because it fails in this way. Besides vaccination in childhood, it is advisable to have it done again when the person is grown up. This is a perfect preservative.

In the Kandyan country, and perhaps in other parts, there is a dewala whose god is supposed to cure itch. As in the case of Pattini, there is no such being. An effectual remedy may be found without leaving home. Itch is caused by a very small insect, somewhat like a louse, burrowing in the skin. Like lice in the head, it generally comes from want of cleanliness. Sulphur ointment, well rubbed over the part, soon ilkls the insect, and cures the disease.

Astrology.

Astrology is a false science which pretends to foretell things by the planets.

Many persons believe that the fertility of the seasons, success in every undertaking, health and sickness depend upon the planets. Hence astrologers are consulted for a lucky time before commencing any business. Farmers ask when they should begin ploughing or sowing: people leaving home on a journey inquire when they should set out; a man wishing to build a house must find out the lucky day and hour; a sick man wishes to know the best time for taking medicine. When a child is born, the astrologer is called to write out his horoscope, foretelling the events of his life. Astrologers are sometimes consulted about marriages. Suitable matches may be broken off, because it is said the planets are unfavourable.

People are put to never-ending expenses in consulting astrologers, and are kept in constant fear lest they should be ruined by the evil influences of the planets. To avert such danger, a *Bali* ceremony is performed by some ignorant tom-tom beater.

Origin of Astrology,—In very early times the sun, moon, and stars were looked upon as powerful gods, and were worshipped. First they were considered to preside over the days of the week. Sunday was under the Sun; Monday, under the Moon; Tuesday, under Budha or Mercury; Wednesday, under Mangala or Mars; Thursday, under Brihaspati, or Jupiter; Friday, under Sukra, or Venus; Saturday, under Sani, or Saturn. Rahu and Ketu were afterwards added, with the Twelve Houses, &c.

Astrology Hurtful.—It is injurious in several ways: There is first the expense of maintaining astrologers who do harm instead of good.

Success in business often depends upon doing things at the right time. A little water will quench a fire at the beginning; but if allowed to go on, all efforts to put it out may be useless. It is somewhat the same with the work of the farmer, the merchant, and every other employment. God has given to each one reason to guide him; but, if instead of using it, he consult an ignorant astrologer, it is not surprising that he should be unsuccessful.

Suppose a man asks an astrologer whether he will gain or lose in a certain undertaking. If the astrologer says he will lose, the man becomes dispirited and fails; whereas if he had been earnest and active, he might have succeeded.

Astrology has a mischievous effect in the case of marriages. Parents in search of a husband for their daughter find a young man suitable in every respect. The horoscopes of both are placed in the hands of an astrologer, and he is asked if they agree. Sometimes he says that if the marriage take place one or other will soon die, or some misfortune will happen to the parents. The daughter may thus get a bad name, and her marriage become very difficult.

Horoscopes pretend to tell how long a person will live. A man promised old age will be unmindful of death, while one whose years are said to be few will be kept in constant fear of the dreaded hour.

Astrologers have been bribed to assert that persons would die at a certain time. Those who gave the money did so with the idea that they would die of fright, and then they would inherit their property.

Under Sinhalese kings, if a child's horoscope was bad, the parents either gave it away or murdered it. No punishment was inflicted for such a crime.

Astrology False.—All enlightened nations of the world now disbelieve in astrology. A Native Almanac is filled with lucky and unlucky times. In an English Almanac not a single entry of this kind is to be found.

The following are some of the reasons why astrology is considered false :—

1. *From the Nature of the Planets.*—As it has been mentioned, the planets were thought to be powerful gods. Surya was supposed to move daily across the sky in a gold car, drawn by seven white horses.

About 200 years ago, an instrument for looking at distant objects, called the telescope, was invented. Some are now made very large—even 40 feet in length, —by means of which the heavenly bodies can be seen far more distinctly than with the naked eye. The sun is known to be merely a large ball of fire, surrounded by blazing clouds. The moon is composed of stone like our earth, with mountains and plains. The world on which we live is a planet.

Kandy is surrounded by hills. It would be foolish to say that the hills determine the fortune of its inhabitants. It is just as absurd to say that lifeless bodies, like the planets, regulate human affairs.

Some say that the planets are God's ministers. Would any king in his senses appoint nine stones to be his ministers? Can we believe the all-wise God to be guilty of such folly?

Rahu and Ketu, supposed to be red and black serpents which try to seize the sun and moon, are mere inventions of ignorant men, having no existence. Only people, who are no better than children, can believe such folly.

2. *Astrology is contradictory.*—People sometimes ask for fortunate days to begin a lawsuit. If both parties consult an astrologer at the same time, they will receive the same answer, although one of them must lose and the other gain. If a queen and the wife of a scavenger each give birth to a son at the same moment, both will be born under the same planets. Their horoscopes should be the same, but how different will be their future lots!

3. *The predictions of Astrologers are nearly always false.*—Some things written in horoscopes come to pass. It may be said of every one born in this world that if he live he will have sickness at some time or other, and that if he recover he will not then die; that he will have seasons of prosperity and adversity; that he will have friends and enemies. These may be safely written in every horoscope. But when astrologers pretend to tell how long a person will live or such things, they are right only in a few cases by chance.

A Native Officer of high rank got his daughter's horoscope written out carefully. Her age was fixed at 60, but she died when 16 years old. An examination of the horoscopes written by the best astrologers has shown that in nearly every case they are wrong. Ignorant people never think of testing horoscopes in this way. If shown to be untrue, the excuse is made that there was some mistake in the birth hour or in the calculation.

4. *The most prosperous nations do not consult astrologers.*—The Queen of England now governs Ceylon, and about 150 princes in India acknowledge her sovereignty. She has no astrologer, while all the kings of Ceylon and Indian Princes had astrologers. English people are richer and more successful in their

undertakings than those who are guided by the planets. Why are astrologers themselves generally poor?

5. *On urgent occasions no one is foolish enough to consult astrologers.*—If a man's house is on fire he does not ask for an auspicious time to put out the flame. In cholera or when bitten by a snake, he applies medicine at once.

The Sin of Astrology.—The great evil of astrology is, that it is a sin against God. It is placing inanimate planets in the room of their Creator.

The one true God is King. He is Lord of heaven above, and of the earth beneath. Agriculture, commerce, government, &c., are all dependent upon His control. Mercury, Mars, Venus, Jupiter, Saturn, the Sun and Moon, are all His servants. They have no authority, not even over the most insignificant things. They are but lifeless bodies, and faith in them is not of the slightest advantage. Let us worship Him alone, who is their and our Creator, the Most High, the Almighty, the Omniscient, the All-holy, the infinitely Just, the All-merciful God.

God never changes, never ceases to reign. No one can usurp His authority. No time is more lucky or unlucky than another. Any time is proper for what ought to be done; but anything wrong is equally forbidden at all times, and the guilty must suffer the consequence.

God has given two great lights to guide us through life—the light of reason and the light of His holy Word, called the Bible.

In the ordinary affairs of life, as the time for ploughing, sowing, &c., we should be guided by reason, after seeking God's direction and blessing. In our moral conduct and in religion, we should be guided by the Bible. It shows how we may be truly happy, both in this life and in that which is to come.

Omens.

These are another kind of fortune-telling as foolish and false as astrology.

Some omens are taken from birds. Crows are favourite prophets.

A man was assured that if he saw a couple of crows the first thing after walking from sleep, he would be lucky the whole day. He therefore ordered his servant to call him as soon as he saw two crows together. The next morning, finding two crows near each other, the servant ran and awoke his master; but before he could come and see them, one of the crows flew away. For this the master whipped the servant, saying, "Ass, why did you not call me before one flew away?" "Sir," replied the man, "I saw two crows and have received a whipping by way of luck. What would have happened to you, I wonder, if you had seen the pair?"

The lizard also bears a high reputation. An Indian treatise on divination says that if a lizard fall on the head, it prognosticates death; if on the right ear, good; on the left ear, evil; on the nose, disease; on the neck, joy, &c. Its chirp is also a certain sign. There is, however, a Tamil proverb, "The lizard which was the oracle of the whole village has fallen into the broth pot."

The ass likewise appropriately holds a place. If an ass bray in the east, success will be delayed; in the south-east, it forebodes death; in the south, it denotes gain of money; in the south-west, good news; in the west, disturbance, &c.

Sneezing, the howling of dogs, &c., are considered to forebode evil tidings.

Even after marriages have been arranged with great trouble, they are sometimes broken off on account of supposed bad omens. The parents, on starting upon a marriage expedition, carefully watch the omens for about half a mile, as if they were infallible indications of the future. If the omens are bad, they return; and if they are bad a second and third time, the match is entirely abandoned as one that would be ruinous.

Through being guided by omens, favourable times

for going on a journey or commencing an undertaking are often lost, and failure is the result.

Omens are childish superstitions. There is not the slightest connexion between meeting a horse or a Brahman and the good success or bad success of any business. A lizard is not a prophet to foretell future events. Can we suppose that God makes known to a dog, a creature without a soul and without reason, what He does not reveal to the wisest men? If the plaintiff and defendant in a suit went to court together, they would meet the same omens, yet one would lose and the other gain the case.

Another false kind of fortune-telling is by looking at the hand.

Dreams are mere idle fancies passing through the mind, and do not mean anything.

Punishment of Fortune-Telling in England.—Astrology and fortune-telling are so well known to be a cheat, that in England any persons taking money in this way are regarded as "rogues and vagabonds," and may be sentenced by a magistrate to imprisonment for three months with hard labour.

The Evil Eye.

Many ignorant persons suppose that the look of a man with an evil eye will render a field or garden unfruitful or do harm in some other way. In gardens, an old pot, spotted with chunam, is sometimes put up to catch the evil eye, and take off its influence from the vegetables. Stories are told about the supposed effects of such looks.

All this is nonsense. Evil eyes have no more influence than charms. It is an ignorant groundless belief. The fields in England produce some of the richest crops in the world, but not in one of them can a pot be seen. Even in Ceylon intelligent people do not follow such a foolish custom, while their gardens bear equally well.

CAUSES OF SICKNESS.

It has been shown that demons neither cause nor cure diseases: hence charms and ceremonies are useless. The chief true causes of sickness will now be mentioned. By guarding against them, people, as a rule, will enjoy excellent health. It is much easier and better to prevent sickness than to cure it.

1. **Bad Water.**—This is one of the principal causes of fever. Decaying things, whether plants or animals, are generally poisonous. The water of marshes in which plants are rotting, is unfit for use. One of the worst kind of fever is brought on by matter from privies soaking into wells. Privies should never be near wells.

If good water cannot be had, the water used should be boiled, which helps to destroy the poison.

2. **Unwholesome Food.**—Special care is needed about food when cholera prevails. Unripe or over-ripe fruit should be avoided. Badly cooked or indigestible food is also hurtful. Too much should not be eaten, especially at night.

3. **Want of Cleanliness.**—"Filth is the mother of sickness." If we go near a dung heap, a stench is perceived. This arises from little particles, given off the decaying matter, being drawn in by our breathing and the nose feeling their touch as a smell. Filth of every kind gives off such unwholesome particles, even though their smell may not be observed. Houses should be whitewashed regularly. Hollows, near houses, where water may lodge, should be filled up. Plantain skins and other refuse, if they cannot be removed, should be thrown into a pit at some distance from the house on the side from which the wind does not generally come.

4. **Insufficient Clothing.**—Cold wind blowing on the body is a frequent cause of fever and other sickness. To keep the belly warm, especially at night, is a great safeguard. Most care is needed when the seasons change.

5. **Neglect of Vaccination.**—As already explained this is the chief cause of small-pox.

Precautions against Fever.—When this disease prevails, be very careful about water. Do not go out in the morning fasting, and take good food in sufficient quantities. Avoid exposure to great fatigue, to the dew, and to night air. Do not sleep in the open air. Wear warmer clothing than usual. Especially keep the body warm at night. Sleep on a bedstead, and not on the ground

Pure air is also of great importance.

By attending to the foregoing directions, much sickness may be prevented.

Conduct in Time of Sickness.

Many diseases can easily be cured by a little care at the beginning. The body, itself, gives help. If dust gets into the eyes, tears begin to flow to wash it out; if we take unwholesome food, sometimes the stomach tries to vomit it, or the bowels seek to get rid of it.

When a person feels ill, he should stop work, and lie down, keeping himself comfortably warm. Instead of his usual meals, let him take conjee or some light food. If this is done, it will often be sufficient to restore him to health.

When cholera prevails, special care is necessary. Some cholera pills should be kept in the house and taken if there are signs of an attack.

When an illness threatens to be serious, get at once a good doctor. Never use charms or ceremonies, and do not employ a doctor who recommends them. They have been shown to be worse than useless.

Little Books on Health.—The directions given here are very short. *The Way to Health,* sold near the Kachcheri, Colombo, (Price 8 cents) contains advice on the subject from some of the best doctors.

There are many foolish and hurtful customs with regard to childbirth. The *billas* of pregnant women are *Kalu Kumara Dewatawa* and *Reeri Yakka.* There are no such beings. A little book on *Childbirth* (price 6 cents), sold at the place above-mentioned, shows what should be done during pregnancy, and how to have safe delivery.

It must be allowed that in some cases the best doctors cannot cure diseases. Every one who is born must die at some time or another. But in fatal diseases demon ceremonies cannot possibly help, and they may hasten death.

How to prevent Fear of Demons.

It has been shown how hurtful, in several respects, demon worship and other superstitions are to the Sinhalese. Every effort should be made to put an end to such false alarms. Education is one of the chief remedies ; good doctors are another. But other means should also be employed.

1. **Parents should never deceive children by false fears.**—The Sinhalese are so much afraid of demons, because from their earliest years people have frightened them by lies about *billas.* Children who have been properly brought up have no fear either of the dark or of demons. Nor is it necessary to tell lies to children to secure their obedience.

2. **The making of Masks should be discouraged.**—Children see them, and the belief is fostered that demons really exist. If all masks were destroyed and none allowed to be made, demon ceremonies would come to an end much sooner.

3. **Trust in God.**—The Sinhalese are frightened by imaginary demons, by omens, &c., because they do not worship the Almighty Creator and Preserver of the Universe. It is a great sin to forsake Him and bow down to images that can neither see nor hear, or to make offerings to demons.

God alone is Lord of life and death. At the same time He is our Father in Heaven, and loves us like a father. We have been disobedient children, forsaking our true Father, and joining His enemies. He earnestly calls us to return. Confessing your past misconduct, go to Him asking forgiveness. To enable Him to pardon us, He gave His Son Jesus Christ to die for us. Taking refuge in Him, we shall be safe. And let us ask Him to send His Holy Spirit to purify our hearts, and make us fit to dwell with Him for ever in heaven.

A child is not afraid to go along any road holding his father's hand; so, trusting in God, we need not fear what any one can do to us.

The Bible tells us about Satan and other evil spirits; but they are quite different from the yakkas of whom the Sinhalese stand in fear. They do not cause disease, but tempt men to sin. God can protect us also from these.

Prayer to God is the only effectual charm.

Some ignorant people are afraid that if they gave up ceremonies, the demons would injure them. If children had used *billa* ceremonies and discontinued them, would any harm befall them? No, because there are no *billas*. It is the same with demon ceremonies. There are no demons to harm people.

DUTY OF EDUCATED SINHALESE.

Demon worship, as has been mentioned, is the religion of savages. There are some Sinhalese still so barbarous that in cases of sickness they do not give medicine, but simply resort to charms and devil dances.

Others, not quite so rude, give medicines, but also employ ceremonies, as they think the former alone insufficient. Most Sinhalese belong to this class.

Mr. Dandris de Silva Guneratne, Modliar, writing in 1865, thought that not more than four or five hundred Sinhalese in the whole Island did not believe in charms. The number is larger now, but still it is lamentably small.

Educated Sinhalese should do all in their power to

put an end to demon ceremonies and other superstitions.

Ignorant women are the chief supporters of such customs. They wish them observed through love to the sick person in hope of a cure. But if an unskilful person tries to give medicines to a sick person, he may do much harm. Wisdom is necessary as well as love. It should be explained that such ceremonies are useless and hurtful, and their performance should be positively forbidden in every case. Charms should be broken off. At the same time, a good doctor should be employed, and God's blessing sought.

One of the most common excuses for demon ceremonies is, that they are the custom. Simply to follow the example of our forefathers would put an end to all improvement. In worldly matters people are not so foolish. It was the custom for the Sinhalese to have only jungle paths, and to do all their journeys on foot. Instead of following the example of their ancestors, they are now carried swiftly and pleasantly by rail. Formerly all books had to be written; now the Sinhalese have printing presses; formerly there were no Sinhalese newspapers; should people refuse to read them now?

By seeking the enlightenment of their countrymen, educated Sinhalese will be a blessing to the Island. The large collection of masks used in demon ceremonies, exhibited in the Colombo Museum, is a sad proof of the barbarism of the majority of the population. Kattadiyas, kapuas and others who get a living by such practices will do all they can to oppose them, but truth will triumph in the end. The English, when savages, formerly believed in demons; the belief in them will similarly pass away among the Sinhalese. Let all seek to hasten the downfall of superstition.

A *Billa* to frighten Sinhalese Women.